First Learners

Picture Word Book

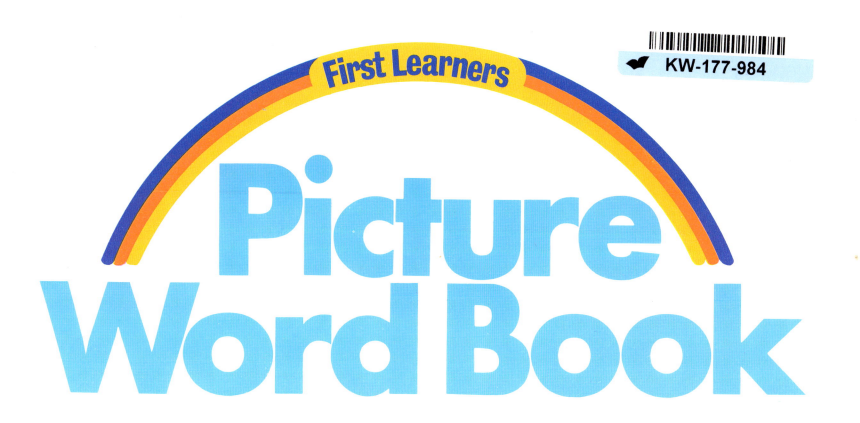

Angela Royston

Illustrators
Colin and Moira Maclean, Liz Graham-Yooll

Consultant
Betty Root

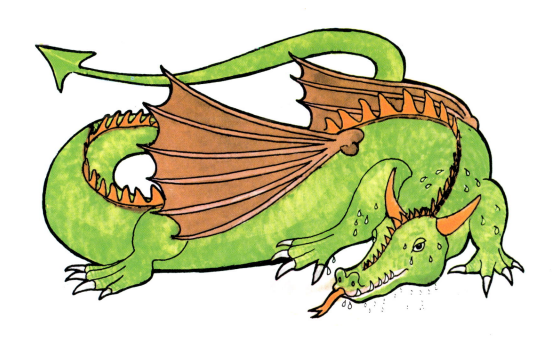

A a

aerial

alligator

This agitated alligator has an aching tooth.

accident

aeroplane

ambulance

The ambulance rushes to the accident.

acrobat

Ann is an agile acrobat.

airport

Aircraft take off and land at an airport.
How many aircraft can you see?

acting

We are acting in a play.

Cover designed by John Strange

Designed and produced for Marks and Spencer p.l.c.
by Grisewood & Dempsey Limited,
Elsley Court, 20-22 Great Titchfield Street, London W1

© Grisewood & Dempsey Limited 1982

ISBN 0 906279 21 6

Phototypeset by
Southern Positives and Negatives (SPAN),
Lingfield, Surrey, England
Printed in Italy
by Vallardi Industrie Grafiche, Milan

anchor

anorak

ape

angel

ant

An ant is amazingly small.

The angry ape jumps
on the ant hill.

animal

A dog is an animal.
There are more animals
on the next page.

antelopes

Antelopes are very shy.

apple

ankle

antlers

apron

Animals

The cows, the pigs and the sheep belong to the farm.
Who do you think the horse, the dog and the cat belong to?
How many pigs can you see?
Who are the squirrel and fox watching?
What is the hedgehog doing?
Which animals do you like best?

crow

sheep

pigs

squirrel

fox

cat

horse

dog

cows

butterfly

hedgehog

worm

fishes

birds

insects

These are all animals too.

monkeys

leopard

ostriches

rhinoceroses

giraffes

zebras

antelope

All these animals live in Africa.
They live on the great grassy plains.
Which animals have stripes?
The stripes help them to hide
in the long grass.
The giraffes are the tallest animals.
They can reach the leaves on the trees.
What are the zebras doing?
Who is asleep in the tree?
Who else is in the tree?
How many birds can you see?

reptiles

shellfish

worms

aquarium

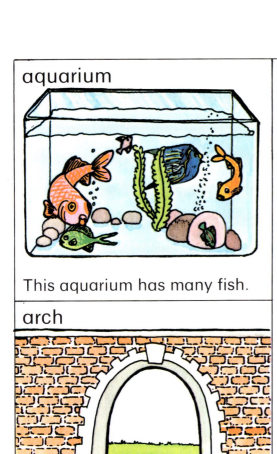

This aquarium has many fish.

arch

armour

Sir Alan is wearing armour.
Arrows cannot harm him.

arrows

artist

Alistair is
an absent-minded artist.

armadillo

arms

I have two arms.

armchair

Archie is asleep
in the armchair.

arrow

airport

This arrow shows the way
to the airport.

astronaut

autumn

In autumn the leaves fall from the trees.

avalanche

The avalanche has blocked the road.

axe

All the animals are in the ark.
The armadillo is late.
Can you help him find the way?

a b c d e f g h i j k l m n o p q r s t u v w x y z

B b

balloon

bear

baby

This bawling baby
is wearing a blue bonnet.

banana

beavers

Beavers break up branches
to build their dam.

bag

The bag is full of bottles.

barge

ball

Belinda is bouncing
a rubber ball.

bath

Barry is having a bubble bath.

bed

bees

The bees buzz around Bill's bald head.

bicycle

birthday

Barbara is six today. She is having a birthday party.

birds

The birds battle for bacon rind on the bird table.

biscuits

Which biscuits do you like best?

bone

boat

bonfire

The bonfire is burning brightly.

boy

This boy is called Bobby.

bricks

book

Brenda is reading a book.

Spooky Tales

bread

bridge

bottle

breakfast

Beth likes a big breakfast.

bucket

boxers

budgie

My budgie is called Bill.

bulldozer

The bulldozer has bumped into the wrong building.

butter

bus

butterfly

This beautiful butterfly balances on a blackberry.

Bill is a burglar
with a bag full of booty.
How many things
in the picture
begin with b?

a b c d e f g h i j k l m n o p q r s t u v w x y z

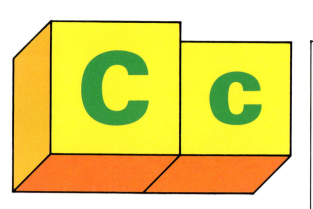

C c

car

cake

Carol's cake has four candles.

caravan

carrying

Colin is carrying his case.

camel

The camel carefully crunches a cracker.

carnival

camera

castle

chimpanzee

The cheeky chimpanzee loves chewing gum.

cat

My cat is very clean.

cheese

chocolate

caterpillar

The caterpillar crawls across the cabbage leaf.

cherries

Christmas tree

cement-mixer

chicken

Sometimes we have roast chicken on Sundays.

church

circle

clowns

The crazy clowns play in the circus.

climbing

Caroline is climbing the chestnut tree.

coat

cowboy

clock

What is the time?

conker

The best conker wins.

The cowboy cannot catch the cow.

clouds

cow

The clumsy cow has crushed the cardboard box.

crab

crane

crocodile

crown

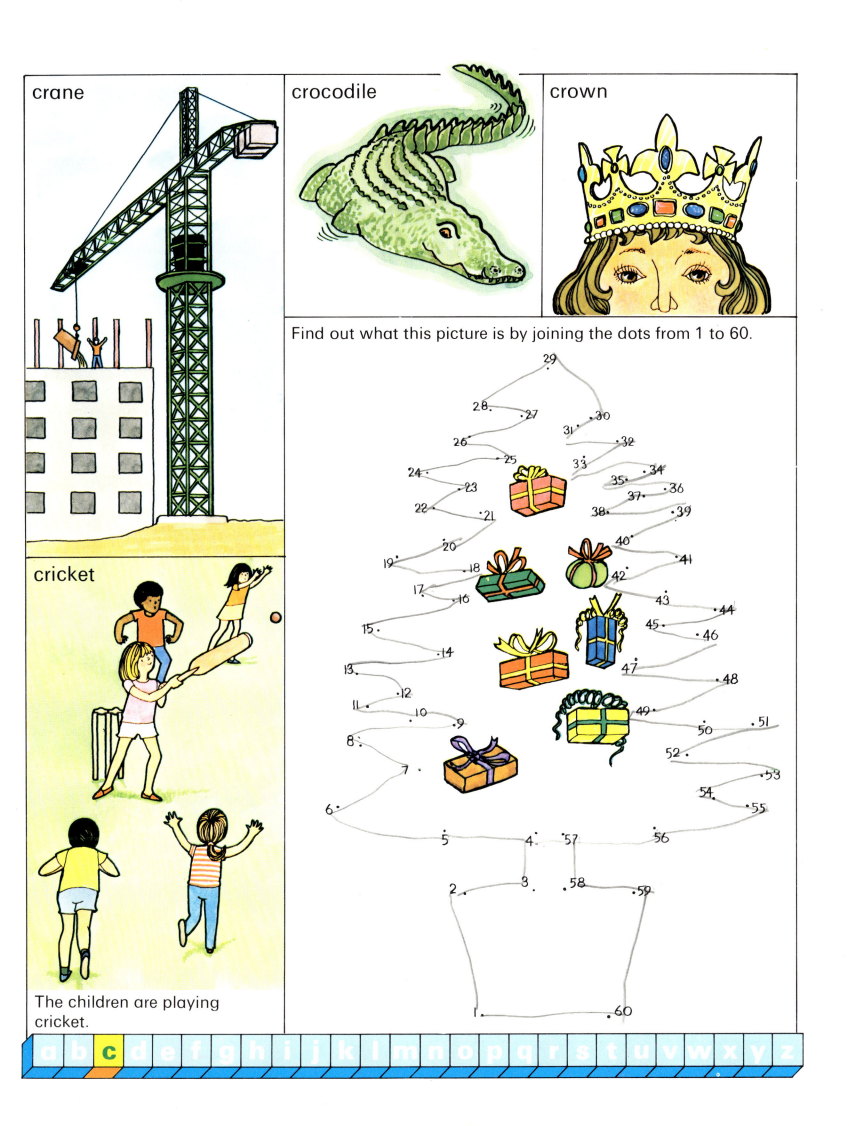

Find out what this picture is by joining the dots from 1 to 60.

29
28. • 27
• 30
31.
26 • 25
• 32
24. 33. • 34
• 23 35. • 34
22. 37. • 36
• 21 38. • 39
19. • 20 40.
• 18 • 41
17. • 16 42.
15. 43
• 14 45. • 44
13 • 46
• 12 47
11. • 10 • 9 • 48
8. 49.
7. 50. • 51
6. 52.
• 53
5. 4. • 57 56 54.
• 55
2. 3. • 58 • 59
1. • 60

cricket

The children are playing cricket.

a b **c** d e f g h i j k l m n o p q r s t u v w x y z

D d

dentist

dinner

daisy

Debbie is making
a daisy chain.

desert

A desert is very dry.

dinosaur

dancer

diamond

Diana has a diamond ring.

Diplodocus was
the longest dinosaur.

dandelion

digging

diving

doctor

I go to the doctor
when I am ill.

dragon

The dreadful dragon drips and dribbles.

dog

The deaf dog
is digging up the dahlias.

dragonfly

dress

Denise has a new dress.

doll

drawers

drilling

donkey

The difficult donkey drops his driver in the ditch.

drinking

driving

Mum is driving us to school.

duck

The dirty duck
dances in the mud.

dustbin

drums

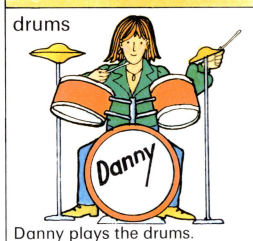

Danny plays the drums.

dumper truck

DINOSAUR QUIZ

Find each of these dinosaurs
in the picture:

 Brachiosaurus
25 metres long, ate plants,
weighed 80 tonnes

 Diplodocus
27 metres long, ate plants,
weighed 10 tonnes

 Ornithomimus
4 metres long, ate plants
and meat, weighed $\frac{1}{4}$ tonne

 Triceratops
8 metres long, ate plants,
weighed 8 tonnes

 Tyrannosaurus
16 metres long, ate meat,
weighed 7 tonnes

 Stegosaurus
$6\frac{1}{2}$ metres long, ate plants,
weighed 3 tonnes

Which is the longest dinosaur?
Which is the heaviest dinosaur?
Which dinosaurs ate meat?

E e

eating

What is Eddie eating?

envelope

eagle

egg

escalator

Earth

We all live on planet Earth.

elephant

This enormous elephant can easily eat eleven eccles cakes.

Eskimo

Eric the Eskimo enjoys jellied eels.

Easter egg

Emma has an exciting Easter egg.

eyes

Elizabeth has blue eyes.

a b c d **e** f g h i j k l m n o p q r s t u v w x y z

F f

farm

factory

This factory makes fireplaces.

farmer

Fred the farmer falls over the fat pig.

fence

fighting

Fiona and Frank are fighting.

fair

fairy

feathers

fire

fire engine

The fire engine rushes to the fire.   The firemen put out the flames.

fountain

fireworks

flowers

fox

The fat fox scratches
a flea in its fur.

fish

This fish has frilly fins.

fly

The fly flits around the food.

frog

The fearless frog leaps
from flower to flower.

flag

footballer

Fergus wants to be
a famous footballer.

fruit

G g

garage
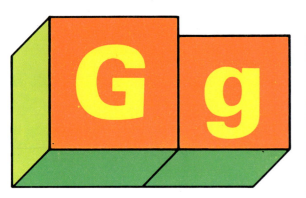

garden

Graham is digging in his garden.

gate

gerbils

giant

George the Giant has great big gumboots.

giraffe

girl

This giggling girl is wearing Granny's glasses.

glasses

glasses

goat

This greedy goat is gobbling the geraniums.

goggles

goose

growing
– 7 yrs
– 6 yrs
– 5 yrs
– 4 yrs

goldfish

greenhouse

Geraniums and grapes
are growing in the greenhouse.

guitar

Here is a picture for you to colour.   g = green   r = red   y = yellow   b = blue
br = brown   p = purple   o = orange

a b c d e f **g** h i j k l m n o p q r s t u v w x y z

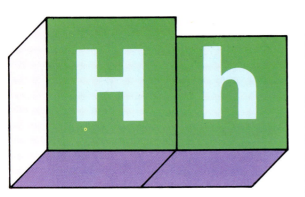

H h

hamster

helmet

hair
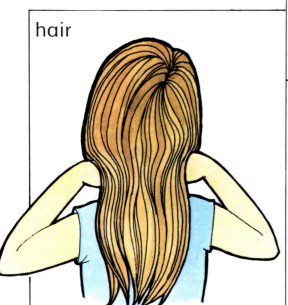

hat

Harriet is wearing
a hideous hat.

hen
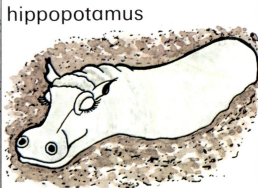

hamburger

Hungry Harry has
a huge hamburger.

hedgehog

The hopeful hedgehog
hunts among the holly.

hippopotamus

The happy hippopotamus
hides in the mud.

hammer
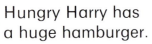

helicopter

horses

The horses hurry home for hay.

house

hovercraft

hospital

Helen visits her Granny in hospital.

hyacinth

A hedgehog, a fox, a frog, a hen, a sheep and a mouse are hiding in the farmyard. Can you find them all?

a b c d e f g **h** i j k l m n o p q r s t u v w x y z

My House

This is our house.
Mum is cooking in the kitchen.
She is making breakfast for us.
What can you see on the table?
Paul is looking in the fridge?
What could he be looking for?

roof

Bathroom
blind
pot plant
toilet
Me
basin
bath
bath mat
towel

Landing
door
bannisters

Kitchen
cupboard
fridge
pans
iron
sink
Paul
table
stool
cooker
Mum
floor

Hall
stairs

gate
lawn
swing
path
drain

I am washing my face in the bathroom.
How many things in the bathroom
begin with b?

Helen is getting up. What time is it?
What can you see on her dressing table?

Dad is in the sitting room.
What could he be looking for?

Tom is Paul's friend. He lives next door.
What is he doing?
What can you see in the garden?

Bedroom

wardrobe

Helen

lamp   bed

mirror

rug

slippers   dressing table

drainpipe

window

Tom

Sitting room

bookcase

lamp

picture

chair

fireplace
radiator

sofa

Dad   table   carpet

hedge

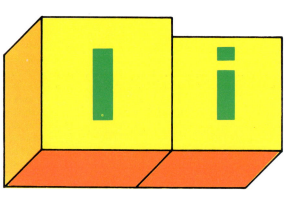

I i

igloo

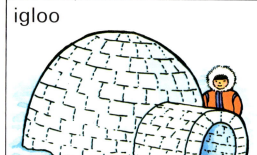

An igloo is
a house made of snow.

insect

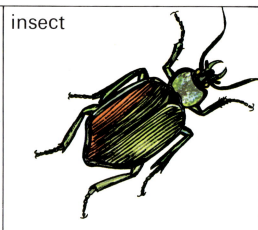

ice

When it is very cold,
water turns to ice.

ink

island

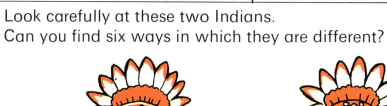

iceberg

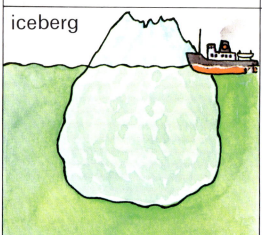

Look carefully at these two Indians.
Can you find six ways in which they are different?

ice-cream

This is a chocolate ice-cream.
Which flavour
do you like best?

a b c d e f g h **i** j k l m n o p q r s t u v w x y z

J j

jockey

The jockey rides in a race.

juice

Janice is drinking orange juice.

jeans

juggernaut

jumbo

This jigsaw makes a big jumbo.

jelly

juggler

This jolly juggler has dropped a jar of jam.

jumping

Jack is jumping over Jane.

jellyfish

junk

a b c d e f g h i j k l m n o p q r s t u v w x y z

K k

kangaroo
Kangaroos can jump a long way.

kicking
Katie is kicking the can.

kissing

kilt

kite

kettle

king
The king looks at his kingdom from the keep of his castle.

kitten

key

kiwi
A kiwi cannot fly.

knife

knitting

koala bears

knight

knot

This knight is knock-kneed.

Katie is tying a knot in her handkerchief.

The children's kites have become knotted. Try to sort them out.

Karen Keith Kitty Ken Kate Karl

a b c d e f g h i j **k** l m n o p q r s t u v w x y z

L l

lanterns

letter

ladder

leaves

light bulb

lambs

lemonade

lighthouse

lamp

leopard

The lazy leopard
lies among the leaves.

The lighthouse flashes
in the dark.

lion

The lion loves to roar loudly.

llama

The llama has long eyelashes.

lumberjack

lizard

lorry

LONG LASTING LAMPS and LIGHTS LTD

LIZARDS AND LADDERS
Play this game like snakes and ladders.
You go down the lizards and up the ladders.

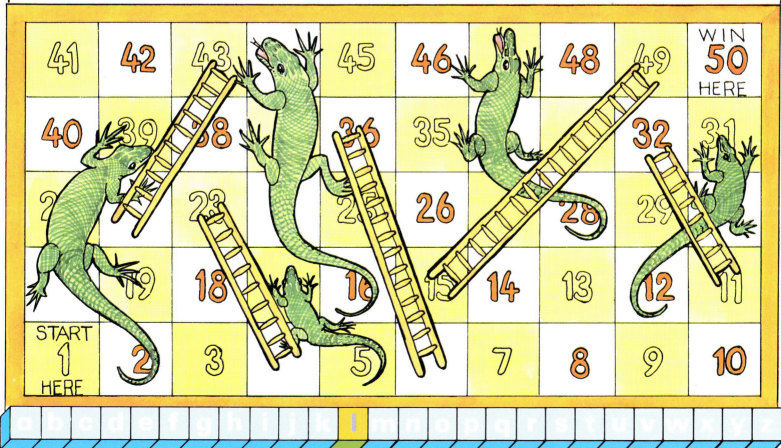

a b c d e f g h i j k l m n o p q r s t u v w x y z

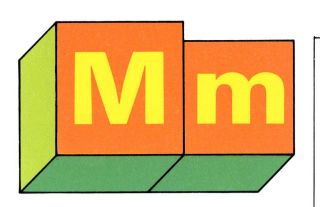

Mm

map

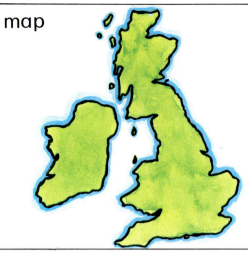

match

The children are playing in a football match.

magnet

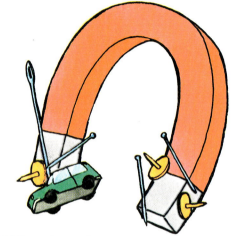

What has the magnet picked up?

marbles

medal

Maurice has won a medal for the most magnificent moustache.

mammoth

This mighty mammoth roamed the Earth almost a million years ago.

market

We are shopping in the market.

match

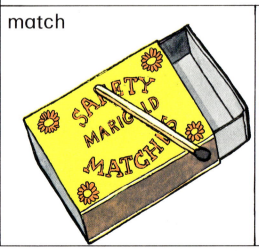

melon

milk

monster

Some people think there is a monster in Loch Ness.

miner

This miner digs for coal under the ground.

Moon

mountain

money

mosque

mouse

The muddled mouse mistakes her home.

monkey

The mischievous monkey mixes milk with the marmalade.

motorbike

mug

a b c d e f g h i j k l **m** n o p q r s t u v w x y z

Myself and My Family

head
shoulder
back
arm
waist
wrist
leg
heel

hair
forehead
ear
eyebrow
nose
eye
cheek
mouth
chin

face
neck
chest
elbow
thumb
fingers
hand
thigh
knee
shin
foot
ankle
toes

My clothes

anorak

vest

jersey

coat

shirt

tights

t-shirt

pants

shoes

jeans

socks

pyjamas

skirt

dress

Dad

Auntie Mary

Uncle Peter

Mum

Grandad

Penny (cousin)

Steve (baby brother)

Me

David (cousin)

Granny

Pussy

Diana (sister)

Mike (brother)

Rover

We have some visitors. Who are they?
What is Penny carrying?
What is Granny doing?
What is Grandad wearing?
What are Diana and Mike doing?
What is Pussy doing?
What is Rover doing?
Do you have any brothers or sisters?
How many cousins do you have?

N n

nails

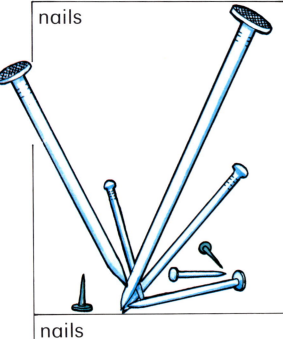

nest

nettles

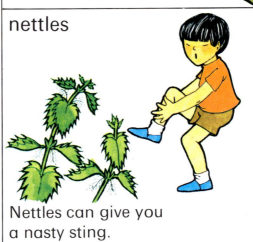

Nettles can give you a nasty sting.

nurse

nails

newspaper

nuts

necklace

Nasreen has a necklace made from nuts.

night

At night I can see the Moon and stars.

a b c d e f g h i j k l m **n** o p q r s t u v w x y z

O o

orang-utan

The gentle orang-utan swings in the trees.

ostrich

The enormous ostrich is an odd-looking bird.

octopus

How many arms has an octopus?

organ

Oliver plays the organ.

owl

The owl hoots and howls at night.

onion

orange

Find the pairs of words that rhyme.

a b c d e f g h i j k l m n o p q r s t u v w x y z

P p

PRETTY POLLY!

panda

The panda pats the pine cone with her paw.

parrot

The parrot perches on the plant pot.

paddling

Pippa is paddling in the pool.

parachute

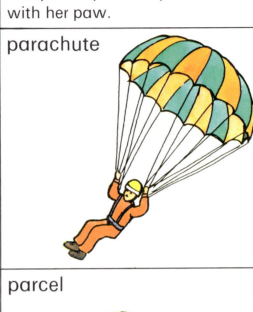

peacock

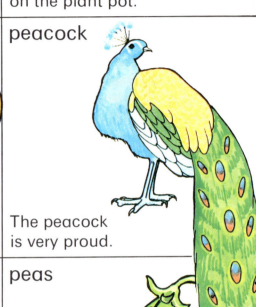

The peacock is very proud.

padlock

parcel

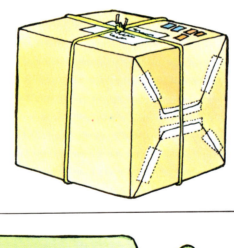

peas

palace

penguins

penknife

picture

policeman

The policeman picks up a possible clue.

photograph

Who is in the photograph?

pineapple

postman

The postman brings a parcel for Praveel.

piano

Peter plays the piano.

pirate

pyjamas

picnic

pyramid

p

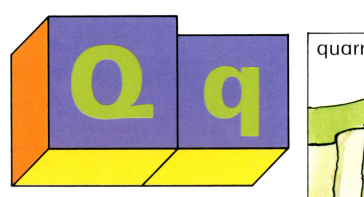

quads

These quads all look alike.

quarry

queen

The queen holds a quacking duck.

queue

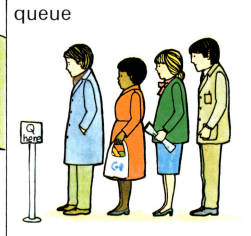

quilt

These quads should all look the same.
Fill in the things which are missing.

Alice   Beth   Carol   Diana

a b c d e f g h i j k l m n o p **q** r s t u v w x y z

R r

radio

razor

rabbit

The frightened rabbit rushes to its burrow.

railway station

race

Richard and Rachel are running a race.

rain

record

Ruth puts a record on the record player.

radiator

rainbow

How many colours are in the rainbow?

reindeer

road sign

This road sign says stop.

rhinoceros

The rhinoceros
is rough and wrinkled.

ring

robin

ribbons

I have red ribbons
in my hair.

river

rocket

riding

Ron is riding bareback.

road

rod

Robby sets off
with his fishing rod.

roofs

rubbish

roller skating

rope

All these things
are made of rope.

rugby

rose

running

Rosemary is running
round the rose bush.

rolling pin

roundabout

Rebecca and Roy are riding on the roundabout.

abcdefghijklmnopqr stuvwxyz

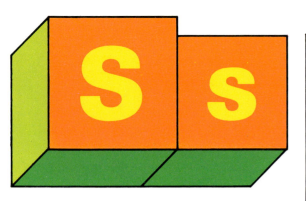

S s

school

sandwich

What is in the sandwich?

scissors

seal

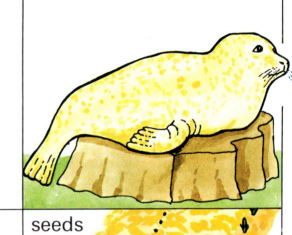

sari

scowling

seeds

These seeds
will grow into plants.

scales

seagull

shadow

My shadow is very long.

shark

This shark has several very sharp teeth.

skunk

A skunk can make a very nasty smell.

sheep

The sheep shivers in the snow.

sings

Susannah sings a sad song.

skyscraper

ship

skaters

signal

skeleton

sledge

Simon's sledge slides down the snowy slope.

At the Seaside

How many people are swimming in the sea?
What has Ben caught in his net?
What is John doing?
Which children are playing with
a bucket or spade?
What is Alex doing?
What is Carol doing?

sunshade

pier

snorkel

seaweed

deckchair

flippers

Steve

sand
pie

sand

Paul

sand
castle

Ben

Sylvia

bucket

spade

net

Peter

crab

seagull

John

shells

How many seagulls can you see?
Who is eating an icecream?
Who is having his photo taken?
Why do you think Jill is wrapped in a towel?
What are Barbara, Debbie and Sheila doing?
How many things can you see in the picture beginning with s?

yacht

windsurfer

sea

water skier

swimmer

Tom

Jill

towel

Carol

Alex

Sheila

sunhat

Debbie

Miranda

Barbara

snail

sofa

spaceman

snake

The snake slithers through the grass.

soldier

spices

nutmeg ginger cloves

snow

spacecraft

spider

snowman

Sharon is making a snowman.

This spacecraft landed on the Moon.

spring

spring

In spring the trees and flowers begin to bud.

submarine

A submarine goes under the sea.

square

stork

summer

squirrel

storm

In summer it is sometimes hot and sunny.

The squirrel nibbles a nut.

stamp

strawberries

sun

sunflower

swallow

swimming

supermarket

Sam is shopping in the supermarket.

swing

Steve is sitting on the swing.

How many things in the picture begin with s?

a b c d e f g h i j k l m n o p q r **s** t u v w x y z

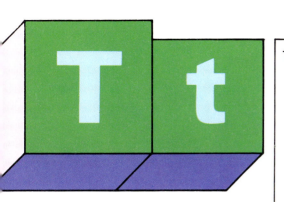

T t

tea

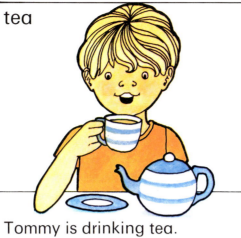

Tommy is drinking tea.

telescope

Tessa peers through the telescope.

tadpoles

One day these tadpoles will turn into frogs.

teacher

television

tank

teeth

Tracy has pulled out one of her teeth.

tennis

Tina and Trevor are playing tennis.

tape-recorder

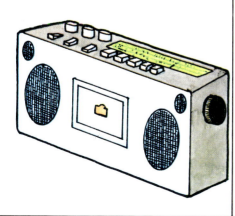

telephone

tent

thermometer

tortoise

Thomas the tortoise takes his time.

train

Tim has a toy train.

tiger

treasure

The treasure tumbles from the tall chest.

tomato

toucan

tools

Can you name these tools?

tractor

tree

trumpet

Tony plays the trumpet.

tug

The tiny tug tows
the tremendous tanker.

triangle

t-shirt

typewriter

Who finds the treasure?

Tom

Tina

Tracy

Trevor

Travelling on Transport

This is a busy street full of traffic.
There are many vehicles shown
in this picture.
Look for the aeroplane in the sky.
How many cars, buses, lorries and vans
can you see?
What other kinds of vehicle are shown?
Which vehicles have been stopped
at the traffic lights?
How many people are crossing the road?
How many other people can you see?

windscreen

bonnet

head
light

number
plate

bumper

bus

scooter

car wash

motor
bike

petrol
pumps

boot

tyre

petrol
cap

aeroplane

train

car

coach

traffic
lights

bicycle

lorry

van

pedestrian
crossing

pavement

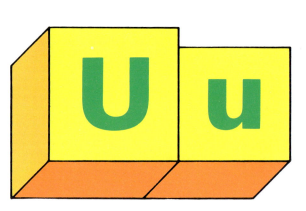

U u

unicorn

usherette

umbrella

The rain cannot get under my umbrella.

uniforms

Who wears these uniforms?

There are ten deliberate mistakes in this picture.
Can you find all of them?

Bakers

V v

van

vet

A vet looks after sick animals.

violin

Valerie plays the violin.

vine

The vine grows up the house.

volcano

Hot rock and ashes spill from the volcano.

vase

violets

vegetables

Can you name these vegetables? Which do you like best?

vulture

This ugly vulture is called Vernon.

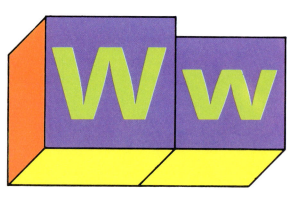

W w

wasp

weasel

waiter

The waiter is bringing our food.

watch

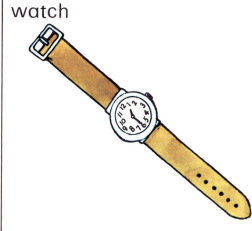

weathervane

The weathervane points to the west.

walking stick

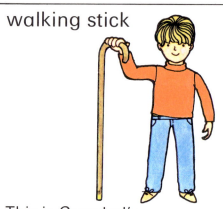

This is Grandad's walking stick.

waterfall

weaving

wall

web

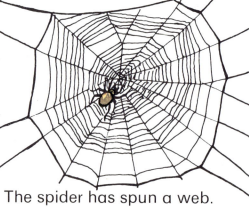

The spider has spun a web.

wedding

whistle

winter

wellington boots

Walter makes
his wellington boots wet.

wigwam

In winter the weather is cold.
Many trees are bare.

whale

The biggest animal is a whale.

wolf

The wolf watches
the wriggling worm.

wheel

windmill

The wind turns the sails
of the windmill.

wrestlers

a b c d e f g h i j k l m n o p q r s t u v w x y z

X x Y y

yashmak

X-ray

An X-ray shows the inside of my body.

yacht

yoghurt

xylophone

yak

The yak has a shaggy coat to keep it warm.

yoyo

105

195

There are six differences between these pictures. Can you spot all of them?

a b c d e f g h i j k l m n o p q r s t u v w x y z

Z z

zebra

zoo

Name these animals.

zigzag

This path has many zigzags.

zip

Dizzy Lizzy is lost in the zigzag maze.
Can you help her find her way out?

WAY OUT

Numbers

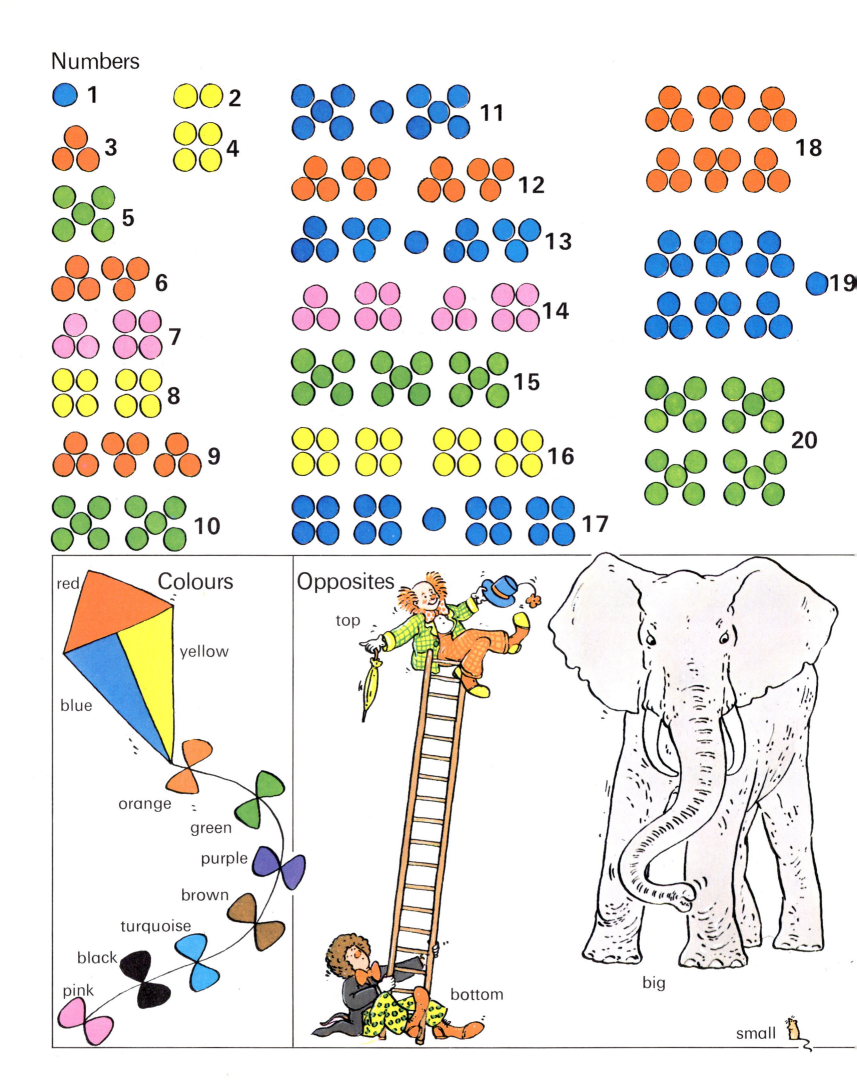

1 2 3 4 5 6 7 8 9 10 11 12 13 14 15 16 17 18 19 20

Colours

red
yellow
blue
orange
green
purple
brown
turquoise
black
pink

Opposites

top
bottom

big

small

Answers to puzzles

Burglar Bill
There are 18 things beginning with b.
They are bicycle, boots, brakes, beads,
ball, bangle, banana, belt, binoculars,
box, bowl, badge, bun, bell, bottle,
book, beans, brush.

Dinosaur quiz
Diplodocus is the longest dinosaur.
Brachiosaurus is the heaviest dinosaur.
Ornithomimus and Tyrannosaurus ate
meat.

Red Indians
The Indian on the left has
1. a short blue tassel with
2. a green circle at the top.
3. His hand is open.
4. He has 17 feathers in his head-dress.
5. He has no white dots on his
head-dress.
6. The stripes on his legs are red,
blue and green with blue in the middle.

Knotted kites
Karen has a blue kite
shaped like a bird.
Keith has a green kite.

Kitty has a red kite.
Ken has an orange box kite.
Kate has a yellow kite.
Karl has a pale blue kite.

Rhyming pairs
The words that rhyme are
mouse and house,
sock and clock,
book and hook,
carrot and parrot.

Identical quads
Alice needs a bangle, lace on her
sleeves, and a white belt.
Beth needs two clasps in her hair,
a necklace, a stripe round the
bottom of her dress, and socks.
Carol needs a bangle,
lace on her sleeves and on her collar,
another button, and a stripe round
the bottom of her dress.
Diana needs two clasps in her hair,
and a collar with lace round it.

Snow scene
Things beginning wth s are sledge
snow, seagull, sun, skates, scarf,

snowball, spots, snowman, spider, sky.

Treasure hunt
Trevor finds the treasure.

Deliberate mistakes
1. Girl is posting a cabbage.
2. Boy is rowing a boat up the street.
3. Strawberries are growing on a tree.
4. The baker's shop is selling clothes.
5. The plant is upside-down.
6. The orange light on the zebra
crossing is square.
7. There are no road marks for the
zebra crossing.
8. A pig is driving the car.
9. The car has a square wheel.
10. The policeman is wearing the
wrong hat.

Identical yachts
The first picture has
1. a different number on the sail,
2. no mast on the ship,
3. a person missing on the yacht,
4. an extra sail on the yacht,
5. a lighthouse on the cliff,
6. no smoke from the ship.